# Introduction

It may seem strange to have an Irishman writing a book about tramways on the Isle of Man, and even more unusual for an Irish publisher to bring out a railway book on a non-Irish subject. However, since English publishers frequently bring out books on Irish railway subjects, it does no harm to turn the tables once in a while, perhaps not for the last time!

I first fell in love with the Isle of Man when, as a young teacher, I accompanied a number of school day trips from Belfast to Peel, and hence Douglas and Castletown in the early 1980s. On these visits, I took more than a passing interest in the Douglas Horse Trams, but I was primarily interested in the steam railway and the electric line up to Laxey and Ramsey.

Like most people, I presumed there wasn't a lot to horse trams, but that was before I discovered the Fintona Horse Tram. Fintona is a village of some 2000 people located near my home town of Omagh, Co. Tyrone. Its main claim to fame was its horse tram which, up to its closure in 1957, was not only the last horse tram in Ireland (by 38 years) but the last in the British Isles to run a daily service in all four seasons of the year. Douglas had ceased to offer this facility back in the 1920s.

In 1992, as Chairman of the West Tyrone Historical Society, I undertook to research and write a detailed history of the Fintona Horse Tram. This I enjoyed immensely, and from the experience I developed an interest in trams in general and horse trams in particular. In Fintona I discovered that a tram horse was not just a horse, but *Dick*. When I came to the Isle of Man to study the Douglas Horse Trams in 1993 I discovered that tram horses were not just horses but 'trammers' and might be *Danny*, *Margaret*, *Sonny*, *Vorrey* or even *Norman*.

I read everything I could find about the Douglas trams, but apart from *Tramways of the Isle of Man Revisited* by Roy and Nigel Coates, most of them failed to make any mention of the horses and concentrated instead on the trams. In this book, I have determined to redress this imbalance and give the Douglas horses their rightful place. Horses, like people, have personalities and no two of the horses are alike in appearance or temperament. The horses are the motive power of the trams and as such deserve a ...... locomotive does on a railway.

It is not widely realised that horse trams needed about seven horses to every tram, so a fleet of 100 trams required something in the region of 750 horses to operate them. At present Douglas has 41 horses to cover all operating requirements including sickness and 'off days'. Although there is a fleet of 20 active trams, some only run on special occasions, and the fleet includes a range of types to cover all possible weather conditions from heatwave to downpour.

The normal ten minute interval service requires four trams to be in motion at any one moment. Each operating horse works a two hour shift, representing three round trips of approximately three miles, or a total working day of about 10 miles. This means that on any one day around 19 horses will be required to operate the service, equivalent to 5 horses per tram.

Since the horses work only four months in the year, and work only two hours on the days that they do work, the Douglas horses are, by the standards of most working horses, onto a very cushy number here! Cart horses back in the 1930s would have thought nothing of a working day of 10 hours and 20-25 miles, often more, six days a week, all year, and for 15 years or more.

Douglas tram staff might be interested to know that *Dick*, the Fintona horse, worked the service entirely on his own, six days a week all year! There were 11 workings to and from Fintona Junction, a distance of about 1100 yards, translating into nearly 14 miles a day. This is not all that much more than the mileage worked each day by the Douglas horses, with the added benefit for *Dick* that there was gap of 40-60 minutes between each run. However, in fairness to *Dick* it should be said that the Fintona tram, seating 48, was much heavier than any of the Douglas vehicles, and moreover the climb out of Fintona was very much uphill, with occasionally an additional ½ ton wagon laden with heavy boxes on tow as well.

Douglas tram horses begin their working life at the age of four, and are expected to work for 15 years on average. They

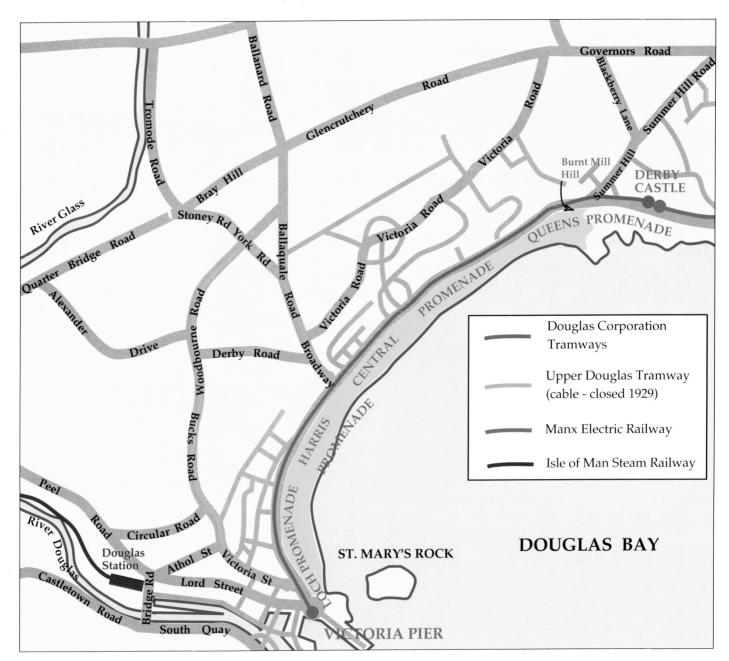

Governors Road

Ballanard Road

Tromode Road

Glencrutchery Road

Victoria Road

Blackberry Lane

Summer Hill Road

Bray Hill

Burnt Mill Hill

Summer Hill

DERBY CASTLE

River Glass

Stoney Rd York Rd

Victoria Road

Victoria Road

QUEENS PROMENADE

Quarter Bridge Road

Ballaquale Road

Victoria Road

PROMENADE

Alexander Drive

Woodbourne Road

Derby Road

Broadway

CENTRAL PROMENADE

HARRIS PROMENADE

Bucks Road

Peel Road

Circular Road

LOCH PROMENADE

River Douglas

Douglas Station

Athol St

Victoria St

ST. MARY'S ROCK

DOUGLAS BAY

Castletown Road

Bridge Rd

Lord Street

South Quay

VICTORIA PIER

Douglas Corporation Tramways

Upper Douglas Tramway (cable - closed 1929)

Manx Electric Railway

Isle of Man Steam Railway

then pass on to happy retirement at the idyllic Home of Rest for Old Horses at Richmond Hill, west of Douglas. Here there are 50 retired horses and donkeys, the oldest of which — *Alfie*, *Rupert*, and *Tony* — have been on the books for around 20 years and enjoy every minute of it! Some horses have a much shorter working life. It depends on factors such as health and aptitute for tram work. Back in Fintona (where every successive horse was called *Dick*), the last horse had worked on the tram for 12 years solid, rain, hail or shine.

The 20 remaining horse trams, out of an original fleet of 50, fall into four different categories. For very hot weather, the most suitable are the open toastracks, so called because of their cross bench seating facing the direction of travel, and their complete lack of any weather protection. These six vehicles are Nos. 12, 21, 38, 39, 40 and 42, and, with the exception of the first one, seat forty on ten benches. No. 12 has only eight benches, thus seating thirtytwo. These cars have a wheelbase of 4' 4". Nos. 21 and 38 are currently in the special blue and gold 'Douglas 2000' livery.

Intermediate in weather protection are the nine bulkhead cars, Nos. 32-37, and 43-45. The bulkhead cars have a roof and are protected by glass screens at each end. However,

**Graham Glover walking *Danny* from the stables to Derby Castle.**

they are entirely open at the sides so that on a sunny day the passengers can enjoy the sea air, but are not overly upset by a light shower. Bulkhead trams have the same seating as the toastracks with thirtytwo seats in Nos. 32-35, and 37; and forty seats in Nos. 36, and 43-45. Most of these very popular cars have a 5' 3" wheel base, though Nos. 43-45 are only 4' 8". These cars are painted in the standard Douglas Corporation livery of signal red and white, as are most of the toastracks. The only

exception to this is No.44, which has been honoured with a special livery on account of it being known as the 'Royal Car'.

The four winter saloons, Nos. 1 and 27-29 are, of course, not used in the winter at all. They are single deck, fully enclosed cars, and provide ideal vehicles for use on wet or very cold days. The winter saloons are finished in cream livery, with red end panels and window frames, and are attractively lined out with the coat of arms of Douglas Corporation. The cars seat thirty on longitudinal benches facing inwards, and whilst Nos. 27-29 are of identical design, No. 1, the newest car on the tramway, is distinctly different and somewhat taller. These cars have a wheelbase of almost 5' 0".

The final tram in the fleet is No. 18 which is unique in several respects. It is the only double deck car in the fleet and is in fact a rebuild of a single deck winter saloon to recreate a type which was common in Douglas in the early days of the tramway. Nos.1-8, 13-18 were originally double deck trams (the second batch being second hand acquisitions in 1887. Most of these had been withdrawn by 1945 and the last was taken out of traffic in 1949. No. 18 ran as a single deck car from 1903 to 1989 when it was converted to its present form. It carries a unique lined maroon livery and comes out on special occasions.

In addition to the active trams, a number of former Douglas tramcars are preserved in other locations, notably double deck car No. 14 in the Manx Museum and bulkhead car No. 46 at Birkenhead Ferry Terminal. Other preserved trams are Nos. 11, 47 and 49. The Tram Shop at Derby Castle was formerly car No. 22.

summer months (May to September). The service commences each morning with the 9.20 from Derby Castle and ends each evening with the 8.30 from Victoria Pier. There are a total of 55 workings in each direction every day with an interval of either 10 or 20 minutes between each tram. There are eight intermediate stops and a trip along the full length of the promenade takes 15-18 minutes, depending on the number of stops.

Horses are usually walked down to Derby Castle terminus from the stables which are located near the bottom of Summerhill Road (see page 3). Sometimes, as shown below, trams are halted on their way to Derby Castle for a changeover of horses near to the stables.

No book on the Douglas Horse Trams would be complete without a brief history of the system. The tramway is the oldest surviving tramway in the British Isles and was opened on 7th August 1876 by Thomas Lightfoot. The gauge of 3 feet was identical to that of the steam railway and of the Irish narrow gauge lines at that time spreading in Co. Antrim.

In 1884 the line was acquired by the Isle of Man Tramways Ltd. who, in 1890, extended the tramway from its original terminus at Burnt Mill Hill to Derby Castle. In 1894 the line was then sold to the Isle of Man Tramways and Electric Power Co. Ltd., who owned the Manx Electric and Snaefell Mountain lines. In 1896 the new company built the present Derby Castle depot and also constructed a cable-hauled tramway route to Upper Douglas. This was opened in August 1896 and was operated by 12 cable cars, one of which is now preserved. (see page 20) The cable cars ran only until 1929.

It was in 1902 that the horse tramway and cable line were acquired by Douglas Corporation, who in the same year extended the horse tramway to Victoria Pier. Several attempts were made to obtain sanction for electrification, but none succeeded.

Although a shadow has from time to time been cast over the future of the Douglas trams, they are now so much a part of the image of Douglas that it would be unthinkable to abandon them. If anything, there is a case for extending the tramway from Victoria Pier to the terminus of the Isle of Man Steam Railway at Bridge Road. At present a passenger arriving at Douglas Railway Station and wishing to continue to Ramsey, faces a long walk to the tram stop at Victoria Pier to get a horse tram. Such an extension would allow continuous rail travel from Port Erin to Ramsey (using three different systems).

With the exception of some taken by Charles Friel in 1986 and 1991, the photographs in this book were all taken by the author during a visit to the Isle of Man in the summer of 1993. I am indebted to Peter Cannon, the Operations Supervisor; Michael Crellin, the Tramway Superintendent; and Wilson Gibb, the retired Manager, for their assistance in compiling this book, which I hope will encourage new interest in the tramway.

**Changeover of horses at the bottom of Summerhill, 1986. Gill Kelly leads *Tommy* away while driver Jack Shuttle and conductor Alan Austin attach *May* to the tram.**

This view encapsulates what the Douglas Corporation Tramway system is all about. Here *Sonny*, hauling tram No. 35 (a G. F. Milnes vehicle of 1896) has just passed through the traffic lights at the bottom of Broadway (seen on the left) and is proceeding into Harris Promenade. The Villa Marina is just on the left. Here the tram has completed about two-thirds of its trip from Derby Castle and is on a slight gradient, as evidenced by the side straps being taut, and the driver not needing to use his brake. The bulkhead trams, nine of which are still in use (32-37, 43-45) are the most popular with both passengers and crew, due to their easy access for boarding and alighting. The conductor, Lennie Cowell, is standing on the running board which allows him easy movement along the tram to collect fares while the vehicle is in motion. To the immediate right of Lennie the lower set of traffic lights is rather unique. They allow a northbound horse tram to proceed forward when the main set of lights is at red. This is because, on this stretch of track, both north and south bound tracks are on the seaward side of the road, and a tram proceeding north will not conflict with traffic emerging from Broadway. The driver of No. 35 is Mike Dunning.

At each end of the 1½ mile trip the horse has to be transferred to the other end of the tram. This usually requires the joint efforts of the driver and conductor. Conductor Mike Dunning is leading *Margaret* and driver Graham Glover is carrying the heavy 'swingle tree' which is just visible behind the horse. 1993 was *Margaret*'s first season on the trams and, like most 'trammers' being broken in, the conductor had to steady her at stops by holding her bridle. The stool carried by Mike is required on the toastrack trams, and most of the bulkhead trams, as there is no bench seat to accommodate the driver. Tram 21, along with No.38 on the adjacent track, is painted in the special blue and gold 'Douglas 2000" livery which it received in 1993. The open toastrack trams, like No. 21, are roofless and have no glass panel between the driver and passenger. Note the special bitumen surface between the rails to create more friction for the horses.

This close up view shows the method of attaching horses to the Douglas trams. This operation is performed by the drivers with impressive speed. Essentially this system is very simple compared to Victorian horse tram systems a century ago. The metal swingle tree rests on the tram itself and is retained by a pin which not only secures it, but pivots it as well to facilitate the tram negotiating curves. Short chains with coil springs link the traces to the swingle tree and allow the horse to pull the tram. Tram 35 is about to be hauled by *Helen* and the driver is again Mike. A century ago, trams used a heavy wooden 'tree' which

hung loose, being attached to the horse by leather straps and to the tram by chains. This older system was much more cumbersome and had the disadvantage (for the horse) that the tree kept bumping against its rear legs.

Also visible in this photograph is the brake lever which operates the brakes by tensioning a chain attached under the vehicle to a central pivot which applies the brakes evenly to all four wheels. This system was invented by John Stephenson, an Irish emigrant to America who in 1832 applied it first to streetcars in New York.

This view, taken on the same occasion as that on page 6, shows Mike adjusting *Margaret*'s bridle. The left hand trace (strap) has already been attached but the right hand one is still draped over *Margaret*'s back. Passengers waiting to board trams at Derby Castle are advised to keep clear of the tracks by the yellow line shown. This may seem an unnecessary precaution for such a slow moving vehicle, but the sound of approaching horse hooves is often drowned out by passing road traffic. Starting a horse tram used to require a considerable force for the horse but all Douglas trams now have roller-bearing axle boxes which make it much easier. One of the fawn horses, *Sonny*, has learned how to lean forward against his harness so that the tram moves before he takes his first step, but some horses make harder work of it than others.

*Left:* This view, looking along the Central Promenade in Douglas in 1986, is taken just north of the location on page 5. The southbound horse approaching at a trot is *Alec* driven by Andrew Jepson. No. 34, is one of the thirtytwo seater 1896 bulkheads, and the photograph is taken through the glass of a northbound bulkhead. Note the remains of the trailing crossover visible behind No. 34. These are no longer used. At busy times of the day, trams run at 10 minute intervals, and in the far distance the preceding northbound service is just visible.

This photograph shows very clearly how the Douglas horsetrams occupy the centre of the road, and overtaking vehicular traffic must therefore pass on the inside. Local car owners are well used to this, but visitors in hired vehicles (or their own) need to exercise extreme caution at tram stops to prevent hitting passengers.                          C P Friel

*Right:* The ample backside in this picture belongs to *Tim* and captures perfectly the undulating motion of a horse hauling a tram. The driver communicates his wishes to the horse through the reins, and by a series of whistles. The view is from tram 36, which is a good tram for forward shots as it has a bench seat ahead of the partition. No 36 thus provides the opportunity for 'footplate' trips (if you talk nicely to the driver!)

Just visible on the left is a combined bus and tram stop, though passengers on this occasion are taking little interest in the tram. The tram stop sign is to the left of and just above the yellow 'no waiting' sign on the lamp post. The view here is in Loch Promenade with the Villa Marina Gardens on the right.

The unique winter tram No. 1 approaching Derby Castle Depot in heavy rain. Contrary to what its number suggests, No. 1 is the newest horse tram in Douglas, not the oldest. It was built by J.C. Milnes-Voss in 1913, and has a slightly flatter roof than the other winter saloons (see opposite) and a more pronounced clerestory. In fact No. 1 is considerably taller than the other trams, and this is evidenced in the height of the eight side windows. Graham Glover is protected from the rain by the usual red cape, and *Michael* is leaning forward into the traces as he heads for his rest point.

The front screen of No. 1 is finished in cream and black rather than varnished wood. All four winter saloons have a very fine livery of lined out cream, with red end panels. For a few months in 1983 this car was borrowed by Sealink and after a repaint by Lancaster City Transport, was displayed on the British mainland for promotional purposes.

A very confident looking *Sonny* (see caption on page 8) seems to be having no difficulty with tram 29 as he trots along Loch Promenade on a very wet August morning with a southbound working. Drivers in these weather conditions are provided with highly visible red capes. These not only keep the rain off drivers in their exposed forward driving position, but make them more conspicuous to passing motorists. Trams 27-29 are identical saloon vehicles and date from 1892. With the exception of Nos. 12 and 21 they are the oldest cars in regular use. The protective grill around the running gear means that the wheels of a Douglas horse tram are rarely on public view, but for those curious on this subject, turn to page 23. The white markings on the road occur near certain tram stops and define areas out of bounds to motorists.

A group of suitably clad passengers boarding winter saloon No. 27 on a southbound working along Central Promenade. Like all enclosed tramcars, Nos. 27-29 can only to be boarded at the rear. This is the main reason for their lack of popularity among the crews as they are slower to board and the collection of fares is slightly more difficult than on the toastrack or bulk-head trams. The blue and white diagonal arrow at the rear of the tram indicates to motorists that they should only overtake on the inside. Notice how the brass brake handle is kept highly polished. The external condition of tram 27 with its white roof and varnished wood weather screens is absolutely superb. These cars also carry the Douglas Corporation coat of arms.

The interiors of trams 27-29 are very different from the toastrack cars with their front facing bench seats. These winter saloons have longitudinal bench seats in traditional Victorian horse tram fashion. These cars are nicely panelled and my personal preference is for this design of car, which has so much of the ambience of a traditional urban tram. In theory each bench seats fifteen, but the varying sizes of customers can reduce the total seating capacity below its nominal thirty. The interior design does leave it more difficult for the conductor since he has nothing to either lean against or hold on to, when he is dispensing tickets. The value to the driver of the four legged stool (and the cape) are evident in this view, passing the roundabout at the start of Loch Promenade on a northbound trip. The tram has just set off from the Victoria Pier terminus.

This view of bulkhead tram No. 33 was taken back in 1986, and shows the turnaround at the Victoria Pier end of the journey. All the bulkhead and toastrack trams are used for advertising, and since no two are exactly alike, it is possible to identify individual trams even when their numbers are obscured, as in this view. Most trams take 15 minutes for the 1½ mile trip, and with 8-9 intermediate stops thrown in, the average speed works out at 6 mph. This view shows the horse harness very clearly. Note how driver John Howell holds the swingle tree well clear of *May*

at the rear. The conductor holding the bridle is Peter Martin. It is interesting that the driver always holds the tree on turnrounds and the conductor leads the horse. The blue and white railway carriage in the background is No. F9. It was used in 1986 for promotion for the Isle of Man Steam Railway. It has since been rebuilt and restored to traffic, and, since 1991, has been in service between Douglas and Port Erin.

C P Friel

On a dullish day in 1991, winter saloon No. 29 sits at its Victoria Pier stop point before its return trip to Derby Castle. The conductor can be seen inside the tram collecting the fare from a passenger. In 1993 the flat rate fare was £1.10 regardless of the number of trips in the course of one day. Concession tickets are available to juveniles, children and other appropriate categories. The ferry terminal building is visible in the left background. Unlike an electric tram, the motive power of a horse tram requires the constant attention of the driver, even during a stop over. Here Alyen Kewley (better known as Syd) keeps *Joey* company, while awaiting departure time. The blue coats worn by the driver and conductor are the standard garb for all but the wettest of weather.

C P Friel

A number of Douglas horse trams are preserved in various locations, but the best known on the island itself is probably No. 14. This tram was one of a batch of six Metropolitan Carriage and Wagon Co. double deckers acquired second-hand in 1887 from South Shields, and numbered 13-18. It was built in 1883 and seats twenty inside, and twentyfour outside passengers. Three of these cars were withdrawn before 1945, and Nos. 14 and 15 succumbed in 1949. However No. 14 was retained and in 1955 was passed to the Museum of British Transport at Clapham, in London, where it was displayed for twentyone years. In 1976 No. 14 returned to the island for the centenary of the horse tramway and took part in the historic cavalcade. Since 1976, No. 14 remained on loan (from the Science Museum), seeing very occasional use. In the winter of 1991 it went on permanent display at its present location, the Manx Museum, off the Kingswood Road, in Douglas.

The Science Museum did not permit the tramway to use No. 14 in regular service, but in 1987 the Manager Mr. Wilson Gibb hit on the idea of converting another of this batch of six into a double decker. No. 18, like 14, had arrived in 1887, but in 1903 it had been converted into a single-deck winter saloon, a guise in which it ran until 1988. Approval for No. 18's reconversion to a double-decker was given by the Town Council in May 1988, and in 1989 No. 18 emerged, looking resplendent in the maroon livery shown here, which was chosen by the sponsors of the conversion, Isle of Man Breweries Ltd. This view shows the author beside No. 18 at Derby Castle depot in August 1993. On this occasion, No. 18 has been taken out especially for the photograph and *Sonny* who had just arrived from the stables to haul a toastrack tram, was somewhat surprised and perplexed to be hitched instead to No. 18 which was not going anywhere!

This interior view of No. 18 shows just what a magnificent vehicle she is and the high standard of her restoration, which was undertaken by Mr Alec Corris. Note the framed photographs displayed above the windows. One interesting detail is that No. 18 has eight windows along each side compared to seven in No. 14. The end doors of the saloon are sliding, a feature which was virtually standard in trams. Having just written a book on the Fintona Horse Tram in Northern Ireland, the previous year, I was particularly interested in this vehicle which was built by the same maker (Metropolitan) and in the same year as the Fintona tram. Visible through the end window is tram No. 12, the last surviving early toastrack, dating from 1882, and built by G F Milnes.

This unusual view show the top deck of No. 18 with Douglas Bay in the background. The ferry terminal which marks the end point of the tramway is visible behind the head of my son. Like most open top double deckers, No. 18 has two longitudinal bench seats facing outwards. Additional seating in the form of a small bench is fitted at each end. The floor of the top deck on vehicles of this kind was cambered steeply to encourage drainage of rain water, and the side sheeting had a gap to permit this to run off the deck. The wooden slats facilitated both drainage and grip. Unfortunately full use can not be made of the large seating capacity of No. 18, because in deference to animal rights supporters who presume that this vehicle is considerably heavier than the bulkhead trams, passengers are restricted to the top deck only, which seats twenty. In actuality, hauling a tram on rails exerts a horse much less than a cart along a tarred road.

This view of Douglas Corporation cable car No. 72 in Derby Castle depot is probably not strictly appropriate to this book, but I have included it on the grounds that it is stored in the horse tram depot, and that like the horse trams, it is not a self-propelled vehicle! The cable system in Douglas came into operation in August 1896 and allowed trams to run to Upper Douglas, from a junction with the horse tramway at Victoria Street up Bucks Road on a gradient (in places) of 1 in 10.6. It then continued up the Woodbourne Road to the Summit at Avondale, before returning to the promenade via York Road (where the tram depot and engine house were located) and Broadway. Cable cars were worked by the tram or car gripping a continuous cable which ran in a central slot between the 3'.0" gauge running tracks (see inset). In Douglas the cable tramway system proved uneconomic and closed in 1929. Fortunately two tram bodies survived, having been made into a dwelling house near Jurby, to the north of the island. In the late 1960s, parts from these were combined to produce today's restored vehicle which is appropriately numbered 72 at one end and 73 at the other.

Both C P Friel

The surviving open toastracks are represented here by No. 38, one of three similar Milnes tramcars, built in 1902 (Nos. 38-40), and seating forty passengers. Here, *Danny* is seen departing from Derby Castle, with conductor Chris Kelly giving a helpful pull to get things moving! The driver is John Howell. The outside seats at the Terminal Bar/Restaurant provide an ideal vantage point from which to view the arrival and departure of both horse and electric trams on a sunny day like this. *Danny* is not the only chestnut horse with white markings, and I am always impressed by the way in which the crew know the identity of all the horses on the tramway. Today only six of the open toastrack trams remain in service — 12 (1882 Milnes), 21 (1890 Milnes), 38-40 (1902 Milnes) and 42 (1905 Milne-Voss). In addition, No. 11 (1886 Starbuck & Co) is preserved in the carriage shed at Douglas Railway Station.

Derby Castle tram depot is a very attractive and well maintained building. The mobile shop, seen here on the right, operates during the horse tram season and is a conversion of open toastrack No. 22 (1890 Milnes), withdrawn from traffic in 1978. From 1884 to 1896 the depot for horse trams was at Burnt Mill Hill, at the bottom of Summerhill Road. When Derby Castle depot opened in 1896 it was originally a single storey building. In 1935 it was altered to the two storey form shown here, with offices upstairs, and the eleven original roads were reduced to nine. The building is well worth a visit, containing trams less regularly seen in use, as well as the cable tram and double deck tram, No. 18.

This interesting view shows the wheel sets from bulkhead tram No. 32 at Derby Castle in August 1993. The tram itself can be seen jacked up in the background, over an inspection pit. The two sets of wheels make an interesting contrast and they may well represent two different makers. One is probably a G. F. Milnes set, and the other Metropolitan or United Electric. The set in the foreground is considerably dished and is twelve spoked. The rear set are oddly seven spoke and are not dished. The axle-boxes have been removed from the dished set, but are still on the set at the rear. To reduce the strain on the horses, the Douglas Horse Trams have roller bearings.

*Left:* As I have stressed in the introduction, horses are central to the whole operation in Douglas and a visit to the stables at the bottom of Summerhill is well worthwhile. The horses are very well cared for and each horse has its own stall with the collar and harness exclusive to it. The stalls are identified by name, and this line up shows *Carol, Walter* and *Barry* on the left, with *Douglas, Pompie, Norman,* and *Angela* on the right.

*Right:* Retired tram horses are in the care of The Home of Rest for Old Horses at Bulrhenny, Richmond Hill, Douglas. In fact the 30 ex-tram horses retired here are close to the numerical strength of the active roster in Douglas itself. The Home has 12 horses and 8 donkeys which are not 'trammers', so all in all there are 50 residents at present. The three happy pensioners in this view are (l-r) *Topsy* (retired 1988), *Ivy* (retired 1985), and *John* (retired 1989). The background scene is looking west across the island towards Foxdale with the Crogga River at the bottom of the field. The Home of Rest for Old Horses is open Monday-Wednesday from late May to mid-September, and admission is free. (Telephone: 01624 674594)